AROUND THE GLOBE

MUST SEE PLACES IN

ASIA

BABY PROFESSOR
EDUCATION KIDS

Asia is the Earth's largest and most populous continent, located primarily in the eastern and northern hemispheres. Given its size and diversity, the concept of Asia—a name dating back to classical antiquity—may actually have more to do with human geography than physical geography. Asia varies greatly across and within its regions with regard to ethnic groups, cultures, environments, economics, historical ties and government systems. Asia is home to several language families and many language isolates. Most Asian countries have more than one language that is natively spoken.

CAMBODIA

officially known as the Kingdom of Cambodia and once known as the Khmer Empire, is a country located in the southern portion of the Indochina Peninsula in Southeast Asia. This was once the seat of one of Asia's most magnificent early civilizations, the mighty Khmer empire of Angkor, whose legendary temples continue to provide a touchstone of national identity – as well as attracting millions of visitors every year. Rural Cambodians wear a krama scarf which is a unique aspect of Cambodian clothing.

is a sovereign state in East Asia. China's landscape is vast and diverse, ranging from forest steppes and the Gobi and Taklamakan deserts in the arid north to subtropical forests in the wetter south. TheHimalaya, Karakoram, Pamir and Tian Shan mountain ranges separate China from South and Central Asia. China is one of 17 megadiverse countries, lying in two of the world's major ecozones: the Palearctic and the Indomalaya. By one measure, China has over 34,687 species of animals and vascular plants, making it the third-most biodiverse country in the world.

CHINA

DUBAI

is the most populous city in the United Arab Emirates(UAE). Dubai has emerged as a global city and business hub of the Middle East and South Asia. As of 2015, Dubai is the 23nd most expensive city in the world and the most expensive city in the Middle East. Dubai has been called the "shopping capital of the Middle East". Dubai has a rich collection of buildings and structures of various architectural styles.

is a country in South Asia. It is the seventh-largest country by area, the second-most populous country with over 1.2 billion people, and the most populous democracy in the world. Home to the ancient Indus Valley Civilisation and a region of historic trade routes and vast empires, the Indian subcontinent was identified with its commercial and cultural wealth for much of its long history. Indian cultural history spans more than 4,500 years. India is notable for its religious diversity, with Hinduism, Buddhism, Sikhism, Islam, Christianity, and Jainism among the nation's major religions.

INDIA

INDONESIA

is a country in South Asia. It is the seventh-largest country by area, the second-most populous country with over 1.2 billion people, and the most populous democracy in the world. Home to the ancient Indus Valley Civilisation and a region of historic trade routes and vast empires, the Indian subcontinent was identified with its commercial and cultural wealth for much of its long history. Indian cultural history spans more than 4,500 years.

is an island nation in East Asia. The Kanji that make up Japan's name mean "sun origin", and Japan is often called the "Land of the Rising Sun". Japan's feudal era was characterized by the emergence and dominance of a ruling class of warriors, the samurai. Japan has a large industrial capacity, and is home to some of the largest and most technologically advanced producers of motor vehicles, electronics, machine tools, steel and nonferrous metals, ships, chemical substances, textiles, and processed foods.

JAPAN

MYANMAR

is a sovereign state in Southeast Asia bordered by Bangladesh, India, China, Laos and Thailand. A diverse range of indigenous cultures exist in Burma, the majority culture is primarily Buddhist and Bamar. Burma is a country rich in jade and gems, oil, natural gas and other mineral resources. Burma's slow economic growth has contributed to the preservation of much of its environment and ecosystems.

is a sovereign state in East Asia, constituting the southern part of theKorean Peninsula. The name Korea is derived from the Kingdom of Goryeo, also spelled as Koryŏ. South Korea's economy was one of the world's fastest-growing from the early 1960s to the late 1990s, and South Korea is still one of the fastest-growing developed countries in the 2000s. South Korea has a technologically advanced transport network consisting of high-speed railways, highways, bus routes, ferry services, and air routes that criss-cross the country.

SOUTH, KOREA

THAILAND

is a country at the centre of the Indochina peninsula in Southeast Asia. Among the ten ASEAN countries, Thailand ranks second in quality of life and the country's HDI (Human Development Index) is rated as "high". Thailand is the 2nd largest economy in Southeast Asia after Indonesia. The elephant is Thailand's national symbol.

is aparliamentary republic largely located in Western Asia with the portion of Eastern Thrace in Southeastern Europe. Turkey is a democratic, secular, unitary, constitutional republic with a diverse cultural heritage. Turkey's growing economy and diplomatic initiatives have led to its recognition as a regional power. Turkey has a sizeable automotive industry, which produced over a million motor vehicles in 2012, ranking as the 17th largest producer in the world. There are 40 national parks, 189 nature parks, 31 nature preserve areas, 80 wildlife protection areas and 109 nature monuments in Turkey.

VIETNAM

is the eastern most country on the Indochina Peninsula in Southeast Asia. Archaeological excavations have revealed the existence of humans in what is now Vietnam as early as the Paleolithic age. Vietnam has been, for much of its history, a predominantly agricultural civilization based on wet rice cultivation. Vietnam's culture has developed over the centuries from indigenous ancient Đông Sơn culture with wet rice agriculture as its economic base.

BẢO TỒN VÀ PHÁT HUY CÁC

SẢN VĂN HOÁ CỦA LỄ HỘI PHỦ DẦY

is a landlocked country in Southeast Asia. Laos' strategy for development is based on generating electricity from its rivers and selling the power to its neighbours, namely Thailand, China, and Vietnam. Its economy is accelerating rapidly with the demands for its metals. Sinh is a traditional garment worn by Laotian women in daily life. It is a hand-woven silk skirt which can identify the woman who wears it in a variety of ways. In particular, it can indicate which region the wearer is from.

LAOS

HONG KONG

is an autonomous territory located on the southern coast of China at the Pearl River Estuary and the South China Sea. Hong Kong is well known for its expansive skyline and deep natural harbour. As one of the world's leading international financial centres, Hong Kong has a major capitalist service economy characterised by low taxation and free trade. Hong Kong is frequently described as a place where "East meets West", reflecting the culture's mix of the territory's Chinese roots with influences from its time as a British colony.

is an Arab kingdom in the Middle East, on the East Bank of the Jordan River. Jordan offers everything from world-class historical and cultural sites like Petra and Jerash to modern entertainment in urban areas most notably Amman. Religion and tradition plays an important part in modern-day Jordanian society. Jordanians live in a relatively traditional society that is increasingly grappling with the effects of globalization. Jordan is considered one of the Arab World's most cosmopolitan countries.

JORDAN